MEOW!

Your Kid's Book About Caring For Cats

From A to Z: The Health, Grooming, Feeding, and Behavior, of your new best friend

By Kina Fisher

CONTENTS

Introduction: Welcome! 1

Chapter One: Unique Personalities of Cats 3

Chapter Two: Taking Your New Cat Home 13

Chapter Three: Mealtime! 23

Chapter Four: Playtime! 29

Chapter Five: Time to Wind Down 33

Chapter Six: Keeping Clean 37

Chapter Seven: Health of your cat 43

Chapter Eight: A lifelong friendship 51

INTRODUCTION:
WELCOME!

Chances are, you've been around cats before.

Maybe your family had one when you were younger. Or a friend or family member had a cat that you remember fondly. You may have even seen cats roaming in your neighborhood!

Cats are unique and curious pets, and it's a great idea to own one.

If you have newly acquired a pet cat or are thinking about getting one, welcome! There is plenty of information in this guide to help you understand and care for a cat.

This book is meant to take you through every aspect of caring for a pet cat. We'll go over what to expect in your first few days. Then, we'll cover what cats eat, how they play, sleep, and clean. Finally, we'll get into how to care for a sick cat.

Are you ready to learn more about the most popular domestic household pet there is?

Let's get started!

CHAPTER ONE:
UNIQUE PERSONALITIES OF CATS

No two cats are alike. You might find that your experience with cats in the past has been calm. Or, you might have seen cats that are aggressive and playful. Cats, like humans, have a unique range of personalities.

Genetics, environment, and life experiences shape a cat's unique personality. That being sats, cats typically fall into one of these dominant traits of personality:

- Social: Some cats are very social and enjoy the company of humans and other cats. They may be very affectionate and enjoy being petted and cuddled.
- Independent: Other cats are more independent and may crave less attention. These cats may prefer to spend time alone and may not show as much affection.
- Playful: Some cats can spend their day chasing toys, playing with strings, or even hunting small animals.

- Curious: Some cats are curious and enjoy exploring their environment. They may enjoy climbing, scratching, and finding new areas to explore.
- Skittish: Some cats can be skittish or nervous, easily scared by loud noises or sudden movements.
- Confident: Some cats are very confident and may not be intimidated by other animals or people.
- Finicky: Some cats can be picky eaters and may not enjoy certain types of food or textures at all.
- Lazy: Some cats may be laid-back and enjoy sleeping or lounging around all day rather than playing or exploring.

Most cats will have a combination of the above traits. For example, a playful cat is usually curious. An independent cat might also sleep all day and be considered lazy.

However, just because a cat is one way, it may not be that way for life. A cat's personality can change over time. For example, a skittish cat can come out of its shell later in life, and the more they feel comfortable and at home. A cat's personality can also change depending on the situation and environment. An owner change or being let outdoors will bring out different aspects of a personality.

Try to take notice of your cat's unique personality. Understanding your cat's personality can help you provide for its needs and improve your bond.

Getting to know your cat in the first few weeks of ownership will be very informative. You will learn how you approach them and care for them throughout their life.

Common cat behaviors

While there is no one typical personality between cats, there are some common behaviors. All of the behaviors below are ones that you may end up seeing in a variety of cats, regardless of their individual personalities.

Grooming

All cats are constant groomers. They will spend a lot of time licking their fur to keep it clean. Cats may also groom other cats as a way to bond. Additionally, grooming can release endorphins in a cat and make them feel soothed.

Cats have a special tongue that helps to remove dirt from their coat. They may groom themselves by licking their fur directly or licking their front paws and then using their paws to clean the rest of their body.

Kneading

Kneading is when cats push their paws in and out against a soft surface. This is usually on a blanket, bed, or a person's lap. You may have heard of it as "making biscuits" because it mirrors how bakers knead the dough for biscuits.

Cats knead as a way to mimic how they used to knead with their paws as kittens to stimulate milk flow from their mother.

Here are a few more reasons why cats knead:

- Comfort: Kneading may show contentment and comfort, as it's often seen when cats are relaxed and happy.
- Marking territory: Cats have scent glands in their paws, and when they knead, they transfer their scent. This could be a way cats mark their territory.
- Stress relief: Kneading can be a form of self-soothing behavior, helping cats calm down and relieve stress.

- Positive feelings: Kneading may be a learned behavior that cats associate with positive experiences, such as being fed or cuddled.

Meowing

You may not know that meowing is not natural for cats. Cats actually evolved to learn to meow to communicate with humans.

You may hear your cat meow at you for a variety of reasons. One, they meow to get your attention. Cats also meow when they want to be fed, petted, or let outside. Cats may also meow to express emotions such as happiness, excitement, distress, or discomfort.

Purring

Cats purr when they are in a relaxed and content state. The exact reason cats purr is not completely known, but it is mostly a sign that your cat is feeling good.

Also, cats can purr in different situations, not only when relaxed. They can purr in pain, stress, or even during grooming. It can be a way they may cope with different situations. For example, purring can also be a form of self-soothing for cats, helping them calm down and relieve stress.

Rubbing

Cats rub their cheeks on many different surfaces, such as furniture, walls, and even people. Cats mostly rub their cheeks on surfaces to mark their territory. When a cat rubs its cheeks on a surface, it transfers its scent from its cheek glands onto the surface.

Cats also rub their cheeks on surfaces as a way of claiming ownership or showing affection. If a cat rubs their cheeks against you, it is a sign it has marked you as theirs.

Cats may also rub their cheeks on surfaces to groom themselves, as they may be trying to remove any loose fur or dirt on their faces.

Warning signs in behaviors

Cats can adapt quickly to living indoors with humans, but keeping your cat well taken care of is essential. If not, they may develop bad habits.

Though uncommon, here are some signs to look out for in your cat that they might be developing destructive behaviors.

Aggression

Cats are emotional creatures and like their routines. Environmental or social changes can trigger extreme behavior. A cat can spit, hiss, and scratch if it becomes fearful. This response can come from new or scary sights, smells, sounds, or animals. The best way to prevent aggressive behavior is to keep your cat indoors and avoid introducing a lot of change if you can.

Scratching

All cats have a natural urge to scratch, which helps to keep their claws healthy and maintain their territory. However, scratching may become a problem around your house if they scratch up your furniture. Destructive scratching can destroy your home and belongings. Provide scratching posts as a positive outlet for scratching, and cover areas of your home or furniture that are off limits to not tempt your cat.

Spraying

Cats may spray urine to mark their territory. An outdoor cat may spray to communicate with other cats as well. If your cat sprays doorframes, curtains, and window ledges inside, it may be responding to a threat outside. Spraying chair legs, beds, and tables can mean your cat is mixing its scent with yours. You can neuter your cat to stop spraying. Or, you can decrease the space your cat has to roam in your house.

Cats versus dogs

Though cats and dogs are the two most common domestic pets, there are not the same. If you've owned a dog before, owning a cat does not necessarily mean you know all there is about owning a pet.

Here are some common differences between cats versus dogs.

Behavior

During the day, dogs are active and playful. While they may take naps, they prefer being with their owners and going on walks. Cats, on the other hand, sleep away much of the day, becoming active right when you're getting ready for bed. In addition to daytime activity, cats and dogs will get your attention with different sounds. While dogs bark loudly or howl, a cat will meow softly to get your attention.

Pack Mentality

Dogs belong to packs and like to work in groups. They tend to see their owner as the pack leader and look to them for direction. Because of this, dogs will insert themselves into your routines as their way of helping you out.

But cats do not hunt in a pack. They are independent creatures who prefer staking prey quietly. They are content spending time alone and don't need to rely on their humans for more than food and a clean litter box. They may still see you more as a motherly figure, however, but come to you for affection and pets instead of guidance.

Bathroom and meals

Cats eat smaller meals and need to eat less than dogs. While cats are meant to only eat and digest meat, dogs are omnivores. This means besides meat, they can eat fruits, vegetables, and grains.

When it comes to the bathroom, cats do not need as much training as dogs. Once a kitten knows how to use a litter box, they should naturally use it whenever they need to relieve themselves.

Dogs mostly relieve themselves outside, though it is possible to house-train a dog to use special bathroom mats indoors. Typically, dogs require their owners to take them out when the need arises, several times a day. With a cat, you'll never know when it's bathroom time, and that's perfectly OK!

CHAPTER TWO:

TAKING YOUR NEW CAT HOME

Getting a cat for the first time

You're ready to take your first cat home – congrats! Cats provide companionship, affection, fun, and entertainment. However, cats are not toys for amusement. They are living creatures that need care and attention.

It is essential to ensure you're willing to provide for its needs first. A commitment to a cat can last up to fifteen years, so consider this first before taking a cat home. If you invest in establishing a relationship with your cat early on, you'll be rewarded with years of happiness together.

In this chapter, we'll explore what you need to do in the first few weeks of owning a cat to prepare yourself and your home.

One cat or two?

One decision you will have to make when bringing a cat home is if you should bring home one or two cats. Of course, two cats can be more responsibility.

However, two cats can also keep each other company and will rely on each other for comfort and entertainment.

In fact, bonded kittens will remain friends forever and do not like to be separated. They'll play together, cuddle for sleep, and even groom one another. It'll also help fight off boredom when no one is home.

If you are adopting a cat and it has a bonded sibling or friend, consider taking both home. It is not a ton of extra responsibility – in fact, you may find you need to entertain your cat less.

If you are getting two cats, it's better to get them together simultaneously. An adult cat used to living alone might not welcome a new cat into the house later in life. If you can take home two furry friends at once, it may prove better in the long term.

First few days

When you first bring home a new cat or two for the first time, there are several things to keep in mind. First, take your cat out of its crate in a small, quiet room so it can adjust appropriately to its new environment. If you have other pets, it's best to let your cat have a room to themselves for the first few days. An extra bathroom or guest room are perfect options.

Watch how your cat interacts with you and anyone else in your home. Vitality and playfulness are indicators of good health. Also, check for a curious attitude. If your new cat wants to explore your surroundings, that's a good thing! They may be extra questioning at first as they smell around and get a sense of the space. Let them roam and try not to discipline them – they will not be that curious forever.

When you bring your new cat home, ensure you are not leaving town anytime soon. This may be the first time your cat is away from its mother and littermates, so it's important to make your cat feel calm, safe, and secure. You might want to sit beside your cat at floor level, so the cat can investigate you and get to know you.

Here are a few more things to keep in mind during the first few days of owning a cat:

- Set up a comfortable and safe room for the cat. Provide a cozy bed, scratching post, litter box, food, and water bowls.
- Introduce the cat to its new home gradually. Give the cat time to adjust to its new

surroundings and slowly allow it to explore the rest of the house.
- Establish a routine. Provide regular meals, playtime, grooming, and other activities to help the cat feel secure and comfortable.
- Provide plenty of positive reinforcement. Reward the cat with treats and praise for good behavior.
- Provide regular veterinary care. Schedule a check-up with a veterinarian as soon as possible to ensure the cat is up to date on care.
- Be patient. Keep in mind that cats are independent and may not adjust to their new home immediately.

Every cat is different and may require various techniques for adjusting to a new home. However, providing a safe environment, a consistent routine, and plenty of love can help your new cat feel at home.

Making your home a safe environment

Before you bring your new cat home, make sure that your home is a safe environment. Cats are naturally curious, so make sure cabinets and garbage are safely secured. You might not even know that many everyday household items, such as cleaning products, cords, and houseplants, are hazardous or toxic to your cat.

High and tight spaces

Cats love to perch up high. It allows them to survey their surroundings and makes them feel secure. A window ledge, tall post, non-slip shelf, or free-standing cupboard are all prime spaces. Plus, a view of the street, backyard, or treetops can keep your cat interested and content for hours.

Cats also love to hide. It allows them to get away from people and other animals. Give your cat an enclosed, private space in a quiet area of the house. Or, you can buy cat tunnels and other toys that promote hiding. Remember to keep cats away from dangerous hiding places such as washing machines, fridges, and dishwashers.

Bedding

Since cats spend most of the day sleeping or napping, make sure their sleeping quarters are cozy and comfortable. Cats love feeling snug and warm, so getting them a basket with a highly padded side or a cushion center is ideal.

Cats prefer soft, warm bedding. Even if you have plenty of cat beds in quiet, sunny spots, your cat may still like your bed, chair, or sofa. It is very tough to train cats not to sleep on the furniture. So, a simple solution is to use washable covers on furniture or shut the doors to rooms you don't want your cat to be in.

Scratching posts

Scratching helps maintain claws and mark territory. Instead of discouraging scratching, redirect it to a scratching post. Some scratching posts can have a perch or a bed on top. Also, you can hang toys from cat scratching posts to give your cat some extra playtime. If your cat does not use the scratching post, try playing with or feeding your cat on it, spraying it with catnip, or placing it near a favorite sleeping area.

Indoors or outdoors?

One thing you may know about cats is that they often like to play outside. However, you may also have seen that it can be quite dangerous for a cat to be out. There are many natural predators of cats. Cats that are allowed to roam can cause disputes between neighbors as well. They may wander onto other properties and spray, fight, defecate, or kill wildlife.

For that reason, most cats are indoors only so they can be safe and loved. Indoor cats are healthier and live longer than their outdoor friends. However, indoor cats will require regular play.

If you feel comfortable letting your cat roam outside, ensure it is safe. Make sure your yard is not a part of another neighborhood cat's territory. Also, make sure your area doesn't include other natural predators for your cat. The first few times your cat goes outside, you may need to accompany them to ensure they are safe. Some owners will use cat bags or leashes to take their cats on walks. It is always good to test the waters and go slow with cats in these outside endeavors.

Also, make sure your yard has no holes or gaps in fences. This is mainly to keep other predators out of your yard. Check your yard for any hazardous plants, such as ivy. Store any pesticides or weedkillers. Make sure there's an easy way for your cat to come back indoors when they're ready.

You can furnish an outside space with weather-resistant scratching poles, beds, tunnels, platforms, and toys. A covered area can contain a regularly-cleaned litter tray and provide protection from the weather. A bowl of fresh water and cat-safe pot plants will complete the space.

Of course, there is no need to put the cat out, which is a common misconception. Keep your cat busy with an exciting environment and fill its physical, mental, and social needs. It will be happy to stay in its home environment.

Handling your cat

It will likely be tempting to want to scoop up and hold your cat once they are in your home. However, remember that your cat is most likely frightened during the first few weeks at home.

Cats generally do not enjoy being picked up and held as much as dogs do. If you've only owned dogs before in the past, keep in mind that this is a different kind of animal with a different personality.

You will need to gain a cat's trust before you can pick them up. Let them come to you and smell you. Then, gently pet them and see how receptive they are. If so, put one hand under the cat's chest, and support its hind legs with your other hand. Lift the cat slowly while holding the cat close to your chest, so they feel secure.

When a cat is in your arms, cradle it against your chest. See how many points of contact you can create between your body and the cat's body. This will make it feel safe and secure. If a cat is struggling in your arms, then put it back down quickly but gently. Maintain your hold on a cat until they are back on the ground to avoid getting scratched.

Training your cat

While cats cannot be trained like dogs, there are some tricks and commands that you can teach them. The first thing you can teach your cat is its name. If you got your cat from a breeder, it would have a registered pedigree name, which can be a lot to remember. An adopted cat from a shelter we already have a name too, and they will recommend that you keep it.

However, it is possible to change your cat's name to one of your choosing. If you change your cat's name, make it a short name. It should be one or two syllables at most. Ruby, Button, and Blue are all great names to give a cat.

It is also OK to get to know your cat first before giving them a name. That way, you can base your name on the personality that emerges from your cat. A cat with a strong personality trait or physical characteristic is a good basis for picking a name. For example, an all-white cat could be named Snowy. One with many markings could be called Spotty.

Remember that, in general, young cats are harder to train because they are easily distracted and have high energy. Be patient with your cat friend if they don't listen to you in the first few weeks.

If you'd like to start training your cat, go slowly. Training sessions should only last a few minutes daily and should take place before meal times. You can command them to come by calling them and shaking a bag of treats. They will be excited by the noise and come to you quickly. When they come to you, give them a treat as a reward. Move to a different position in the house and repeat. Cats respond to positive reinforcement, so they may learn to come during your call sign even without the rattling sound of the package.

Cats are very intelligent and trainable. The secret is finding a reward that they enjoy and keeps motivating them. These are usually their favorite treats or some scratches behind their head.

CHAPTER THREE:
MEALTIME!

Cats do not need to eat as much as dogs, but this does not mean cats do not love food. Much like the unique personalities of cats, a cat's appetite can vary. Some cats love food and will beg for scraps, much like dogs. On the other hand, some cats will not touch human food at all.

Overall, cats who are fed a well-balanced diet are healthier and more content. Cats will adjust their calorie intake to their level of activity. So, monitor your cat's behavior early on to understand its dietary needs.

With that in mind, let's explore in this chapter how to prepare for feeding your cat.

Timing of Meals

You should try to feed your cat at least twice a day at the same time every day. You can feed your cat when it is convenient for you, such as in the morning and around your own dinnertime. An automatic feeder is a good option, so you don't ever forget. You can set the amount of food to dispense at different times of the day.

Since most people spend long hours working outside the home, they may resort to free feeding the cats. Free feeding means the cat has food at its disposal and can eat when it feels hungry. If you. If your cat is prone to weight gain, or if there are other cats around, this might not be a suitable option.

If you take this option, the food should be dry so it will not go bad in the heat. However, if you can, try to establish a feeding routine for your cat. This means you will feed your cat two regular meals a day at the same time every day.

Never feed your cat outside. A food bowl outside can attract stray cats to your garden. This also allows you to monitor how much food your cat eats daily and make appropriate adjustments.

Kinds of foods

Prepared foods (canned, packaged, or dry) contain a mixture of meat, grains, and vegetables. They will provide the right balance of protein, carbohydrates, and vitamins. Cat food will show the labels' nutrients and ingredients, like human food. This will help you make an informed decision.

Additionally, you might see that some cats love to eat grass. Grass does not have nutritional value but can help with digestion. You can buy special cat grass from a pet store, so you do not have to put your cat outside. This is the only kind of plant you should feed your cat. Other plants may be toxic. Make sure you buy special cat grass or a cat-friendly herb like thyme or sage.

Wet versus dry food

Most cats love the flavor and texture of wet food. To add some variety to your cat's diet, you can add wet food and a range of flavors in addition to dry food. There are a variety of types of wet food, such as fish flakes, tuna chunks, minced chicken, and more.

The diversity of wet food ensures that your cat never grows bored with their meals. Make sure you introduce new changes to their diet slowly to avoid upset stomachs.

You can also give fresh or raw food to your cat. However, you should ask your vet or an experienced cat owner first.

Cats can be hesitant to try new foods, so when introducing something new, mix a small amount of it with something you know your cat loves. This also helps to prevent stomach problems when changing your cat's diet.

Treats!

Most cats love getting treats from their owners. There are so many types of cat treats on the market, so choose wisely when picking a new treat for your cat. Look at the nutrition label and make sure that your treat will be a low-calorie snack for your cat. Avoid any treats with high-fat content, and instead, look for high protein. Treats can also help keep teeth and gums healthy. The keyword for all treats is moderation.

Treats can also help promote the hunting instincts in your cat by hiding treats in toys or on high perches. Overall, use treats as a reward, to incentivize play, or to supplement their usual food.

Foods to Avoid

Many common foods are harmful to a cat. In general, it's a good rule to stick to cat food and not feed your cat human food scraps. Do not give your cat cooked bones or chew toy bones, either.

Also, do not mix up foods between your dog and cat, as they have different dietary needs. Cats can't taste sweet things, so there is no need for cat cookies either, even if they're sold from a pet shop.

Water

Since cats are desert animals, they have a low thirst drive. Most of the time, they can get all the water they need from the food they consume. However, you should also provide your cat with a bowl of fresh water at all times, especially if they have a dry food diet. Some cats prefer to drink running water, and they might like to play with your faucet or dripping spout.

Even though some cats enjoy the cool creaminess of milk, it is not an essential part of their diet and can cause stomachaches.

Weight Control

Fussy eaters

If your cat becomes fussy and does not show much interest in their food, try feeding them different flavors and brands of wet food. Most cats respond more positively to wet food than dry kibble, so it's always a safe bet to try that first. Pay attention to when your cat eats, and keep a list of the flavors they seem to enjoy the most.

Another reason your cat may not want to eat their food is if it's in a messy area of your house. Make sure to keep their bowls clean and that area of the house neat and tidy. Remove any scraps of old food and wash the bowl before refilling. If your cat still does not eat, talk to your vet to see if there may be an underlying health issue.

Overeaters

Overeating is not just a human problem; cats can also become overweight. Excess weight places a strain on your cat's joints and organs. It can also affect general well-being and lead to life-shortening conditions, such as diabetes.

You can monitor your cat's weight with regular weighing on household scales. Keeping your cat's weight within a healthy range is suitable for your cat and can avoid unnecessary vet visits.

Growing up

Cats require different diets at different stages of their lives. As a result, as a cat grows older, it might start to require less food. Before adjusting your cat's diet, please speak to your vet to ensure that it gets all the nutrients it needs.

CHAPTER FOUR:

PLAYTIME!

The importance of play

Cats need to play. It fulfills their natural instincts to hunt and explore. Playtime also helps cats stay physically and mentally stimulated. This can prevent behavior problems and promote overall well-being.

Additionally, playing with your cat can help strengthen your bond. Set aside a little time daily to play with your cat.

Kinds of play activities

Toys are a great way to keep your cat entertained. There are a large variety of toys you can buy for your cat. It's best to buy different toys to see which gets your cat's interest. Various play will help keep your cat active, entertained, and happy.

Here are some of the best options to consider:

- Laser pointer: This toy projects a small red dot that cats can chase and pounce on. It's a great way to provide physical and mental stimulation for cats.

- Feather wand: Cats love to chase and catch things that move, and a feather wand is a great way to mimic the movement of prey.
- Ball or bell toys: These simple toys cats can chase and bat around, providing a good workout.
- Interactive puzzle toys: These toys challenge cats to figure out how to get a treat or toy, providing mental stimulation and helping to keep them engaged.
- Automated toys: Some toys, like self-rolling balls, catnip toys, and interactive feeders, can keep cats entertained for hours.
- Hiding and perching spots: A cat tree or cardboard box can provide a hiding spot for cats to relax and watch their surroundings.
- Catnip toys: Some cats respond well to catnip, which can be a great way to engage them and provide stimulation.

You'll find that your cat will often find everyday household items appealing. Items such as paper bags, boxes, balls, paper, or ribbons are often just as appealing to cats. These can be used as play toys, but only under supervision. You can try to maintain your cat's interest in its toys by rotating them out or hiding them.

What not to play with

Your cat will want to play with things that it definitely shouldn't. In fact, as a new cat owner, you may come to find that stuff you leave about the house, such as ties, clips, and lids, may interest your cat the most. For this reason, it's important to tidy up and take care of any choking hazards that seem particularly interesting to your cat.

In addition, don't let your cat play with a new toy unsupervised. Cats have a funny way of doing things you would have never predicted, so always monitor their play first.

Also, do not let your cat play with a person's hands or feet. A cat that plays with hands and feet may not understand the difference between play and aggression. They may continue to bite and scratch even when they are not playing.

Provide your cat with appropriate toys to play with and redirect their play behavior away from their hands and feet. This will help prevent accidental injuries and teach appropriate cat behaviors.

Hunting Hours

Cats are most active during dawn and dusk. This is because many of their natural prey, such as rodents and birds, are also active during these times. Because of this natural instinct, you will find that your cat will want to play more in the morning and after dinner.

Sometimes called the "zoomies," your cat may run around your house and jump from shelves with bursts of energy. It is normal behavior in cats. However, suppose your cat's zoomies are causing problems or becoming excessive. In that case, you may want to consult a veterinarian or a behaviorist. Let your cat exhaust their energy and wind down naturally, which may be hours after you have ended your day.

CHAPTER FIVE:
TIME TO WIND DOWN

Are cats nocturnal?

It's a fair question, considering your cat has zoomies around your house in the middle of the night.

Despite your cat's lack of respect for your sleep schedule, they're not actually nocturnal: they're crepuscular. These are animals whose hours of activity are at dawn and dusk. Crepuscular animals have evolved from desert climates, so they take advantage of when temperatures are the coolest in the desert.

Truly nocturnal animals, such as raccoons and owls, roam throughout the night and take advantage of the darkness to hunt their prey. Crepuscular animals instead take advantage of the fading daylight and darkness to capture the best of both the daytime and nighttime world.

This explains why cats still have slit-shaped eyes, just like nocturnal animals, though they are not truly. This helps them see in the fading light.

Cats and sleep

Cats love to sleep because it is a natural part of their biology. They sleep most of the day to conserve energy for hunting and other activities during their active periods.

The sleep patterns of cats go all the way back to their ancestors, who needed to rest to conserve energy for hunting and avoiding predators.

Cats can also fall asleep and wake quite quickly. Do not be alarmed to see your cat moving around the house in various places for naptime. For example, cats are known to fall asleep perched high on ledges, couches, shelves, and counters. This helps them conserve energy before the hunt.

Do not be concerned that you need to keep quiet around your cat to make sure your cat is getting enough sleep. Your cat will find a corner that suits them and fall back asleep just as if nothing happened.

Cats are always on the alert, even when they're dozing. If a strange noise wakes them, they're instantly aware and fully operational. You may notice this when your cat is in a seemingly deep sleep far away but comes running at the sound of a food container opening.

So, while it may seem like your cat sleeps all day and plays all night, in reality, their schedule just follows a different pattern.

A cat's schedule

Cats typically keep their natural sleep pattern. However, they can adapt to the schedule of their owners to some extent. If you keep your cat indoors, it may adjust its sleep schedule to match yours to some extent, especially if you spend a lot of time with it during the day. But cats will still have their own internal clock, driving their natural sleep patterns and behaviors.

So, cats may be awake when their owners are awake or asleep, but they will not have the same schedule as their owners.

You can gradually adjust your cat's sleep schedule to match your own by making small changes to its daily routine. Here are a few tips that may help:

- Provide plenty of exercise and playtime during the day. A tired cat is more likely to sleep at night.
- Control the lighting in your house. Try to mimic a natural light cycle by providing

bright light during the day and keeping the lights dim at night.
- Feed your cat at consistent times. If you stick to a regular feeding schedule and avoid feeding your cat right before bedtime, they may start to wind down when you do.
- Use positive reinforcement. Reward your cat with treats or playtime when it sleeps during the night.
- Make gradual changes. Try to change the schedule a little bit at a time, moving the schedule by 15-30 minutes each day until the cat is on your sleep schedule.

Cats are independent animals and may not adjust to your schedule easily, so be patient and persistent with the process.

CHAPTER SIX:
KEEPING CLEAN

Cats and bathing

Cats do not need baths like other pets. Cats can clean themselves by licking their fur. Cats have a specialized tongue that helps to remove dirt from their coat. Cats will use their saliva to clean their fur, which acts as a natural conditioner.

Cats like to groom for a few reasons:

1. Cleanliness: Cats spend a lot of time licking their fur to keep it clean and well-groomed. Licking their fur also helps to remove loose hair and dirt.
2. Bonding: Cats also lick each other as a form of social bonding and affection. Licking themselves serves a similar purpose, as it helps them to feel calm and relaxed.
3. Marking territory: Cats have scent glands in their faces and paws, and when they lick themselves, they transfer their scent onto their fur. This helps cats to mark their territory and communicate with other cats.

4. Self-soothing: Licking can also be a way for cats to self-soothe and calm down when feeling anxious or stressed.

It is normal for cats to groom themselves. Still, excessive grooming or licking specific areas can indicate an underlying medical issue and should be checked by a veterinarian.

When to clean your cat

Cats may require regular grooming from their owners to keep their coats and skin healthy. Grooming is an excellent way to bond with your cat and can be very relaxing for them.

Start grooming sessions when your cat is young so it gets used to them. Make the sessions brief and enjoyable. Brush lightly at first with a controlled grip on your cat to make them feel secure. Make sure you are grooming your cat in a calm, relaxed environment. Watch out for any signs of nervousness or discomfort. Establish a weekly grooming routine to keep your cat's coat glossy and in good condition.

Some cats have sensitive areas where they do not like being touched, such as the stomach or base of the tail. Be careful, as touching these areas could trigger an automatic aggressive response.

Include a regular health check in your grooming schedule. Look for anything unusual in your cat's coat or skin during grooming. You should check the following:

- The coat should be soft, clean, and free of knots
- Eyes should be clear and bright
- Ears should be clean, with no discharge or smell
- Teeth should appear free of tartar and gum disease

Check with your vet if you find anything of concern.

Nail clipping

Get your cat into the habit of having its claws trimmed regularly. This is important for indoor cats, who are less likely to wear down their claws. To clip your cat's claws, press gently on each paw pad to expose their claw. Then using your clippers, cut the white tip. Cat clippers are the best and most accurate tools you can use. However, human clippers can be used if necessary with additional care and supervision.

Litter boxes

Training

Most cats will use their little box litter box without much difficulty. Litter training is mostly good timing for an owner. You will have to watch your kitten and wait until it looks ready to use the litter box. This will look as if the cat is raising their tail and crouching down.

When they go to do that, place the box for them to use. Instinct will do the rest. Cats will always cover up their feces, and the smell will guide them to the tray whenever they need to use it. Make sure to reward your kid with praise or treat when they use the litter box at first. This will encourage repeat use.

Scooping

Cats are also very clean animals and will not use dirty litter boxes. Make sure to scoop the litter regularly, if not daily, to keep the box clean and odor free. Dispose of waste in a small waste bag and throw it away.

Kinds of litter

You can use two types of litter boxes: open and covered. Choose the kind you like and stick with it. A cat used to one way or another may be nervous about switching. Ensure the litter box is placed in a quiet corner of your house, far away from the cast feeding area.

You could use several types of litter, from sand, newspaper, wood, or a mixture of various kinds. It's also important to stay consistent with the type of litter you use, or your cat might be averse to using it.

Clumping litter is convenient for scooping. However, what is acceptable for us might not be acceptable for our cats. For example, even though perfumed or scented litter might smell nice to us, it may bother cats and deter them from using the litter box.

CHAPTER SEVEN:
HEALTH OF YOUR CAT

When to go to the veterinarian

As soon as you get your cat, you should book its first vet check-up to ensure they're healthy and happy. Your vet can provide advice on both health and behavior issues. There are there to help you look after your cat, so do not be afraid to ask questions.

After your initial visit, you should visit the vet at least once a year for a wellness exam. Here's what a vet will check during a wellness exam:

- your cat's overall health and weight
- temperature, heart rate, and breathing rate
- eyes, ears, nose, and throat for signs of infection
- vaccinations or flea and tick prevention records

Regular check-ups are an essential part of maintaining your cat's health. Check-ups can help detect and prevent potential health problems.

Outside of these annual visits, you may need to see the vet more depending on your cat's needs and health conditions. Older cats who have health issues or are on medication may need to see a veterinarian a few times a year.

If you notice any unusual signs or symptoms in your cat, you should take it to the vet immediately.

Microchipping

If your new cat does not have a microchip, consider getting one for your initial vet visit. Unlike collars and tags, a microchip is inserted under the cat's skin. Microchipping is the most reliable way of identifying a lost cat. Each microchip has a unique code that can be linked to the contact details of the cat's owner.

If you are afraid microchipping will hurt your cat, don't worry. A microchip is about the size of a grain of rice. The process will not harm your cat.

Vaccines

It would be best to have your cat vaccinated against three fatal cat viruses. These are feline infectious enteritis, feline influenza, and feline leukemia. You should do this even if your cat is indoor only.

If you adopt a cat from a shelter, confirm that all its vaccinations are up-to-date. Most cats get their shots between eight and ten weeks. Throughout the cat's life, it will also need extra boosters during your annual vet visits.

Neutering

To stop the unwanted spread of homeless cats, vets advise your cat to be neutered. Male cats are neutered, and female cats are spayed. Both of these can happen as soon as four months old. Not only do these operations help stop reproduction, but also destructive behaviors. These are routine operations carried out under anesthetic by trained professionals.

Cats will need to rest for several days after a neutering procedure. The recovery time can vary depending on the individual cats, but most cats recover quickly from this operation. Follow the vet's instructions for post-operative care to ensure a smooth recovery.

How to tell your cat is sick

The best way to know when to take your cat to the vet is to understand the signs of a sick cat. Here is what you should look out for if you suspect your cat is sick:

- Changes in appetite. A loss of appetite, or a sudden increase in appetite, can be a sign that something is wrong.
- Changes in behavior. A sick cat may be more tired or less active than usual. It may also hide more often or become more vocal.
- Changes in the appearance of the coat. A dull, matted, or greasy coat can signify illness.
- Changes in the litter box. A cat that is sick may relieve themselves outside of the litter box or use the litter box in smaller amounts.
- Breathing difficulties. Rapid breathing, open-mouthed breathing, or coughing can be signs of a problem.
- Changes in the eyes, ears, nose, or mouth. Discharge, redness, swelling, or any other unusual appearance in those areas can be a sign of infection.
- Changes in weight. Sudden weight loss or gain can be an indicator of underlying health issues.

Cats are good at hiding illness, so it's essential to be familiar with your cat's normal behavior and to pay attention to any change. If you notice any of these signs, or other unusual symptoms, you should take your cat to the vet as soon as possible for an evaluation.

How to approach an injured cat

If you see that your cat is hurt somehow, you may feel like you want to rush to help it. First, before running in, protect yourself! Injured animals often become defensive and may become aggressive to hide their weakness. If you become injured, it will be harder to help your cat.

Approach your cat slowly and calmly, with a soothing voice. Hold your cat tightly to make it feel safe as you look at its injuries. Try wrapping your cat in a large towel or blanket for support. If the wounds can be addressed by a first aid kit (outlined below), ensure you have an adult's support to help. If professional care is needed, contact your vet immediately.

First aid kits

Being prepared with a few basics can help in an emergency situation. Here are a few things to have on hand in case your cat becomes injured:

- Tweezers
- Scissors
- Thermometer
- Roll gauze and gauze sponges
- Adhesive tape
- Antibiotic ointment

- Latex gloves
- A large towel
- A flashlight

Traveling with your cat

When you need to take your cat to the vet or on personal travel, always place your cat in a secure and enclosed carrier. Cat carriers come in various materials. You can find them in plastic, wicker, cardboard, or wire containers. They should be smaller, so your cat feels contained but not suffocated.

Because your cat will most likely use its carrier to visit the vet, it might form a negative association with the carrier. Prevent this by turning the carrier into a safe space. Try leaving it out at all times, with a warm blanket and a few of their favorite treats inside.

General care tips

Here are a few general care tips to keep in mind to ensure your cat has a long and healthy life.

- Avoid over-the-counter flea and tick products. Instead, talk to your vet for safer, more effective, targeted products.

- Always watch your cat when they have a new toy or treat. Make sure they are interacting in their usual way and that they don't have any adverse reactions.
- Avoid feeding your cat table scraps and having them drink from standing bodies of water. Ensure their food and water are refreshed daily to avoid stomach issues.
- Make sure your cat always has updated health records, a list of known allergies, and the name/location of your veterinarian available.
- If you are unsure if your cat has eaten something poisonous, have an adult call the National Poison Control center. You can call 1-888-426-4435 to ask about poisonous effects.

CHAPTER EIGHT:
A LIFELONG FRIENDSHIP

A unique partnership

The bond between cats and humans is unique. In fact, it is considered a one-sided attachment, meaning that it is the human who seeks out the companionship of the cat. Cats are independent animals and do not rely on humans for survival. However, cats can learn to form strong bonds with their human caregivers.

Here are a few of the benefits of cats bonding with their owners and creating a unique partnership:

- Affection. Many cats enjoy being petted and cuddled, so they will seek out human affection for this.
- Companionship. Just as cats like being cuddled, so do owners! Cats can provide comfort and companionship to their human caregivers. This can help to reduce stress and loneliness.
- Shared routines. Cats and humans can begin to develop a shared routine. This can create

a sense of security and familiarity for both you and your cat. For example, you may find they love watching your bathroom morning routine. Or, they may follow you around as soon as you get home every day. Since cats love routine, this can become a reliable comfort.
- Interaction. Cats are very intelligent animals. They can understand human emotions and respond to them accordingly. This can create a deep understanding and interaction between the two species. For example, they might sense when you're sad or scared and come sit on your lap for you to pet them, which they know may help calm you down.
- Mutual benefits. The bond between cats and humans can be mutually beneficial. Cats can provide emotional support and companionship, and humans provide food, shelter, and medical care.

The bond between cats and humans is unique to each individual cat and human. The strength of the bond can vary depending on the personalities of both parties.

For example, your parents or a sibling might have a different relationship with the cat than you do. The cat may be more skittish around a louder, abrasive human, but friendlier around a quiet and calm personality. Pay attention to these bonds to learn more about your cat's inner desires.

The lifelong benefits of cat ownership

The benefits of owning a cat don't dissipate after a few weeks or months. You can come to rely on your cat for companionship, love, entertainment, and affection for its entire life, if you create the right environment.

Consider these unique benefits of owning a cat over other pets:

- They are happy living indoors
- They are neat and groom themselves regularly
- They can use a litter box without training, which is easily cleanable
- They will hunt and kill bugs and pests around your house
- They love to play – with you or by themselves
- They are happy to spend long periods of time alone and can care for themselves
- They are less clumsy than other animals and typically do not make a mess

- They will live happily with kids, cats, and dogs

Next Steps

Now, you may be excited about the idea of bringing home a cat! You've prepared yourself by reading this guide and ensuring you know the basics of cat care.

To help you along with your next steps in the search process, here are a few recommendations:

1. Learn more about the different breeds of cats and their characteristics to find the breed of cat you're most interested in.
2. Research the costs behind many of the tips provided in this book, such as food, litter, veterinary care, and medical expenses.
3. Talk to other cat owners or breeders to get a better idea of what it's like to own a cat.
4. Learn about the local laws and regulations regarding cat ownership in your area. Some areas have restrictions about cats going outdoors. There may also be laws about leashes, licensing, and identification tags.
5. Consider your family's lifestyle and living conditions to have a realistic idea of the commitment of a cat.

6. Start visiting a few shelters or rescue groups to meet cats and see if they are a good match.
7. Once you feel ready, it's as easy as signing some paperwork and learning some tips about your new cat before you and an adult take them home.

Welcome to the wonderful world of cat ownership!

Printed in Great Britain
by Amazon